Diamonds in the Grass

Also by Zenda Vecchio and published by Ginninderra Press

Mavis

A Conversation with Emily

Children at the Gate

Tiger! Tiger!

Light on Dark Water

Becoming Kirsty-Lee

The Swan's Egg

Fractals (Pocket Poets)

Spindrift

Spotted Leaves

Luminous (Picaro Poets)

Zenda Vecchio

Diamonds in the Grass

For Brenda, who keeps on encouraging me

Diamonds in the Grass
ISBN 978 1 76041 397 2
Copyright © text Zenda Vecchio 2017
Cover photo: Dew on green grass © Ruslan Semichev

First published 2017 by
GINNINDERRA PRESS
PO Box 3461 Port Adelaide 5015 Australia
www.ginninderrapress.com.au

Contents

The Quality of Light	7
I Have Found	8
The Flowers You Sent Me	9
Messiah	10
Despair	11
Prism	12
Almost Burnt-out Candle in a Mason Jar	15
Sunday Drive: Early September	16
Gum Tree: Canberra	17
Votive	18
My Mind	20
The Rainbird Tree	21
Bedroom Curtains	22
I Think	23
For My Mother (with regret)	24
Nile Lily	26
Poem for Elwin	27
Poem for Lotte	28
Nature of Light	29
At School	30
Zebra Finches: Mt Barker Fodder Store	32
Poem for Sonja	33
Sometime	34
Tiger Is	35
Through a Window: Tea Tree Gully Library	36
Rare Black Cockatoo	37
Wild Oats	38
On Buying a Bird Bath	40
Lily	42
Poem for Katherine Mansfield	43

On Starting a New Jigsaw: *Lakeside Cottage*	44
Memorial for Bob Snell: Laratinga Wetlands	45
Nectarine Tree in Spring	46
Leaf	47
Magpies	48
In Another Life	49
Turner: *The Bridge of Sighs*	50
Jigsaw: *Sunday Afternoon Teatime*	51
Fifth of August 2015	52
Beginning of September	53
Deer	54
Early Morning	55
Easter Lilies	56
End of November	57
Fantasy in Blue and Silver	58
First Week in September	60
Fantasy in Red and Gold	61
Fusion	62
Laratinga Wetlands	64
Rosellas	65
Poem for the End of Love in November	66
Acknowledgements	67

The Quality of Light

Afternoons the light
Changes
Becomes opaque
Is no longer
Strong enough

The shadows reach
Across the floor

I am defeated

Grief

I have lost too much

Even my hands
In my lap
Are different
An old woman's hands
Not
Surely not
Mine

Enough

Resolutely
I go outside
Refill the bird bath
Watch the sparrows
Come down to
Drink

A kind of peace.

I Have Found

I have found a
New word to
Delight in.

Sunfish.

Not something from the
Ocean
Bright yellow in a
Swirl of silver
Bubbles.

Instead

A plunging wild horse
Distraught rider
All in a haze of
Gold dust.

The Flowers You Sent Me

The flowers you sent me
Are much depleted.

First casualties the
Blue iris and
One small orange gerbera.

To compensate
The lilies have come out
One after the other
Golden lilies (I
Read that somewhere but
I have forgotten now
Its significance)

Above them, proud as
Stags at bay,
The antlered heads of the
Strelitzia.

The last lily bud
Opens.

So innocent.

It does not know it too
Is doomed.

Messiah

He said,
'I am the Light of the
World.'
Held his hands
Out to them
Wanting
(Perhaps)
Reassurance.

But they were
Bedazzled
By their own
Visions
And did not hear
His sadness

He knew

Burning bright
He would
Expend himself
(Oh! so lonely)
To the very end.

Despair

The flame of
My candle
Falters
Then, valiant,
Is soldier-straight
Again.

But it knows

Of course it
Does.

Soon enough
The darkness will
Defeat
Us both

Prism

1

Among the dead
Scattered leaves
A bright red one:

It's remembering
Yesterday's dance.

2

Orange:
Close my eyes and see:

Nasturtiums –
Spill of bright flowers
From a
Hanging basket.

Clivia

Myself a child
Making a
Necklace of
Calendulas.
'Mary's gold,' my sister says
And she's right
Their petals fall
Ingots on the dark
Earth.

3

Yellow is
Sunlight.
Driving with Ros
April and an
Avenue of trees
With sequin-stitched
Leaves.

4

Blue is for the sky

Chicory flowers

Delphinium

At the beach
Rock crabs and a
Child laughing.

5

Green is what
Happens to
Light
When it falls on
Grass.

6

Nothing for indigo
Except the bruised sky
After a violent
Sunset.

7

'Violets for sale
Come buy,
Come buy.'

I turn my head
Away.

Fight pity.

They are so vulnerable
With no leaves
To hide under.

Almost Burnt-out Candle in a Mason Jar

Oh! see her
Dance
My once-bright
Candle-flame

She leaps
Pirouettes
Spins
Oblivious of the
Coming darkness

Such ecstasy!

Behind her
Reflected
In the glass
Her partner shudders
Watches her begin to
Falter.

He'd protect her
If he could.

Sunday Drive: Early September

Sunday afternoon:
Deserted road:
Fenced paddocks:
Little wild plum tree
All alone in the
Wind and the
Rain.

She has such
Dignity.

An illusion perhaps.

But she's determined
To ignore
The torn lace of
Her dress.

Gum Tree: Canberra

Against the pale
Sky
Old tree
Bare branches
Twists of
Witches' fingers.

Along her trunk,
Though,
Strands of bright
Leaves.

She can begin
Now
To crochet
Her own shroud.

Votive

I used to pray
All the time

They said,
'That little girl has
Such faith.'

Not now

Now

Sparrow falls
Broken-winged

Mother chimpanzee
Clutches
Her dead baby

Frightened-eyed the
Children
Huddle in the
Ruins
Of their bombed
Homes

'God,' I whisper,
Desperate,
'God…'

There are no words

Weeping,
I light
Another candle
Maybe it can pray
For all of us.

My Mind

My mind is
Splintering
Into fragments

Shards of glass

Light
(Oh! Light of the
World)
Have pity

For one moment
May they catch
Your radiance
Before they fall

Broken stars
Into the final
Darkness

The Rainbird Tree

Scatter of rocks
And the rainbird tree
Very tall and
Proud.

Below the wild sea:
Spindrift

Above the pinkening
Sky

I have searched for
This place
My whole life through
And never found it.

This morning, though,
I thought I heard a
Rainbird call

Reward enough.

Bedroom Curtains

I remember
The seagulls

Not freewheeling
Wide sky
Magic of sun on
Water

Not them

My seagulls were
Different;
Flew haphazardly
Across grey curtains
Dipped and soared
Above a sea that
Was not there.

Hesitant,
A child then,
I put my hand out
Touched them
One by one

Smiled

Was comforted

The darkening room
No longer
Mattered.

I was not
Alone.

I Think

I think
I am trapped
Inside a
Kaleidoscope

Spinning
Out of control
In a
Spiral of
Light

I am
Red
Blue
Lime-green

Part (perhaps) of a
Mosaic of
Flowers

But

Everything changes

I am nothing now
Nothing

Broken glass

For My Mother (with regret)

I am
Falling
Backwards through time.

Childhood:
Forgotten images

A handful of dried
Pine-fronds

Marigold flowers

A black kitten chasing
Leaves

A broken kaleidoscope

Winter:
Grey water
A piece of red seaweed
Discarded in the foam

School:
Words on a blackboard
A box of coloured
Chalk

A little girl with
White swansdown hair

Frogspawn

A just-born
Poppy flower

And always, always
Each spring
The suddenly tender
Sky.

In all this
I can't find
Your face

I don't know why.

Nile Lily

I think I will
Plant
An agapanthus
In the back garden.
They harbour snails
But oh! The flowers
The very essence of
Blue

Poem for Elwin

Six years old and
He says,
Indignant as a disgruntled farmer,
'Look at the flaming
Galahs.'

I shake my head
Bemused.
Sounds wrong
Flaming's too bright
Is a flaunting of red and
Yellow
Sunset, surely, after a
Hot day.

Galahs are
New-dawn
Rose-pink
Sunrise full of promise.

Poem for Lotte

Almost spring:
The buds of your
Tupelo tree
Will have started
To swell.

I remember autumn:
Bright sky
The heart-red glow of
Its dying leaves.

I hold your
Cold hands
In mine.

What must be,
Must be.

Beauty remains
When all else is
Lost

Nature of Light

Light changes:
I watch it
Awed.

Burns bright
In the heart of
My candle-flame.

Is caught under water
Tangles with sky
And the shuddering
Reflection of
Trees.

Is splintered into
Colour:
Red
Blue
Iridescent purple.
Prism:
Raindrop:
Diamond.

Dawn
Tenderness and
Birdsong.

Silver mist

At night
Pale halo round the moon.
I hold out my hands
To the stars.

At School

At school
They told us about
The blue of Australian skies
But not about the
Birds.

Mornings and the
Silver wings of the galahs
Outlined in light

A lonely kestrel

The simple elegance of
A flight of
Ducks.

Black cockatoos

Spill of finches
To the bird-feeder on
My veranda

Seagulls

And in the evenings
Swoop of the
Barn-swallows

All this:
From dawn to dusk
Australian skies
Mere backdrop
For
Australian birds

James Lister Cuthberton's poem 'The Bush' begins, 'Give me from dawn to dusk/Blue of Australian skies'

Zebra Finches: Mt Barker Fodder Store

Watch them:
Little caged birds
Cocked heads
Bright eyes
Sudden swoop of
Small wings

Hear them:
Continual calling
One to another

A need
(Perhaps)
For reassurance

Or

Or maybe
Something else
Simpler
A longing
For sun and sky
The seeding grasses
Hung with dew

I don't know.

I don't want
To know.

Poem for Sonja

This afternoon
You rang me
'I have a satin
Bowerbird,'
You said
Smug.

Not for much
Longer.

Tonight while you sleep
I will lay a trail
Of enticement:
Blue straws
Turquoise beads from a
Broken necklace
Bic biro tops
Your gate to mine
And
In the morning
Your bowerbird
Will be mine.

Sometime

Sometime
In the night
My candle burnt out

Nothing left now
But a ring of
Amber wax

Tiger Is

Tiger is
Terror in the night
Beauty and power
Majesty.

Lion is different

Waits, sad-eyed,
For another future
Peace on God's
Holy Mountain
Where he will lie down
With the lamb

Not yet though

He is still himself

He stirs;
Below him, on the plain,
Wildebeest
Survival of the fittest
No choice
He must hunt again

Through a Window: Tea Tree Gully Library

Meeting at the library
Too many people
Talking.

Bored I
Stare out of the
Window.

Patchwork sky
After rain

A dark-leafed tree

Burst of light
Oh! look
Two ducks on a
Suddenly silver path

This
Oh! this is
Real.

Rare Black Cockatoo

Rare black cockatoo
At the bird feeder.
No. No.
Ordinary galah
Trick of the light.

Wild Oats

Winter afternoon
She's by the window
Reading

London
Young girl
Her friend,
Laughing,
'Maybe he's the one.
He's had time to sow
His wild oats.'

She stops
Drops her book
Is suddenly
Very cold.

Watches
Light fracture
Into forgotten
Images.

Sees a half-torn
Photograph
Herself a child
Serious-eyed
Uncertain mouth and
Little frightened
Hands.

Her mother's face
So angry:
'I've told you.
Don't ask again.
You don't have a
Father.'

The truth
So simple
She whispers it aloud.

'I was a Wild Oat.'

On Buying a Bird Bath

Months ago
I bought a bird bath:
(Green
Molded plastic.)
Carefully assembled it
(Instructions on the box)
'Product of the UK
Guaranteed to attract
Birds to your garden
Robins, chaffinches
Blue tits…'

Not here yet
Long way to come
Wind and rain
The endless sea.
Soon though,
They'll be here soon,
I have it in writing
More than a promise
A guarantee.

My son says,
Thoughtful,
'What about a birdbath
Made in the USA
That'd bring
Cardinals
Blue jays
Maybe even a
Baltimore oriole.'

I close my eyes
Oh! Oh! delight

Between the branches
Of my flowering trees
(Grevillea
Acacia
Scarlet bottlebrush)
There will be
A kaleidoscope of
Flying birds.

Lily

Early morning and
In my garden
The first just-opened
Lily bud.

She waits
Wine-red with a
Dark heart
Egyptian princess, perhaps,
Sly eyes elongated with
Kohl.

Oh! Oh! already
She has my heart
In thrall.

Poem for Katherine Mansfield

Terminally ill with
Tuberculosis
You wrote,
'On my windowsill
A potted daffodil
Just one but it is
Enough.'

Is it?

Of course.

Already too late for
Hope
There yet remains
Courage.

On Starting a New Jigsaw: *Lakeside Cottage*

My new jigsaw
A jumble of
Coloured pieces
Blue, green, grey
A few pink for the
Climbing roses

I pick up half a
Blackbird
Put it down
Again
Discouraged.

Maybe tomorrow

I've done the
Flying swans
Though
So elegant;
Essential beauty
For a
Chaotic and incomplete
World.

Memorial for Bob Snell: Laratinga Wetlands

This is a good place
Trees and grass
Quiet too
Except for the birds and
The vagrant wind
Among the reeds.

They've made a memorial
For you here
Smoothed a fallen red gum
Engraved a plaque
Your name and the outline of
A spotless crake.

I look for it in
My bird book
'*Potzana tabuensis*
Not only rare but
Unobtrusive.'

The photograph's beautiful
Though

A fitting tribute.

Nectarine Tree in Spring

At last
Spring and a
Suddenly tender sky.

My little nectarine tree,
Half-killed by a
Winter of
Hungry possums,
Puts out a
Handful of tiny
Quivering leaves
And one perfect
Blossom

Leaf

November now:
The trees bright-dressed
For summer.

Grey sky though
Mist of rain
Sudden wind and a leaf,
Confused,
Spirals down.

Oh! Oh!
On the dark road
A green star
Too early
Months too early
For autumn gold.

Magpies

Morning and evening
I feed the magpies
Offer them protection
In my walled garden.

It is simple really.
Retired,
I have become a
Patron of music.

Now all their songs
Belong to me.

In Another Life

In another life
I will give my
Sons
Different names.

Aspen
Kestrel
Marlin

Connect them thus
To
Earth and
Sky and
The turbulent sea

Not much
Perhaps
But a
Beginning
For them and
For me.

Turner: *The Bridge of Sighs*

Anne has bought me
A jigsaw from
The Art Gallery.

Turner:
The Bridge of Sighs.

It's impossible.

But –
Such lovely splotched
Pieces:
Red-brown
Black
Cream

Tomorrow I'm going to
Make them into
A tortoiseshell cat.

Jigsaw: *Sunday Afternoon Teatime*

This morning I arranged
A bowl of
Jigsaw flowers.

We picked them late yesterday
Crossed the wooden bridge
Saw the wild ducks
Shep put up a rabbit
And you called him back
Laughing…

Daisies and anemones
Queen Anne's lace
One wild, red rose.

This afternoon
If I have time
Maybe the tea table
Set with willow pattern plates
A hand-painted jug
Silver spoon.

Shep asleep now
Nose on paws;
In the grate behind him
The fire is a blaze
of orange and red

Oh! Oh! piece by slow piece
I am building for myself
Another, kinder world.

Fifth of August 2015

August:
Wild sky
Wind
A lash of rain.

Under the bridge
The creek
An angry swirl of
Brown water.

But soon
Sweet spring

This morning
Blackbird singing
And a
Pink-blossomed tree.

Beginning of September

Look!
By the galvanised fence
Little wild plum tree
In flower for the
First time.

She trembles in the
Wind
A scatter of
Delicate petals

This is her
Coming of age and
Well she knows it

Deer

My new jigsaw:
BBC 500 pieces
Precious Earth.

For two weeks
I have been a
Sika deer
Shoulder high in
Meadow grass and
White daisies.

Poised
Wide-eyed
Waiting my cue

Not dance or song
Simple elegance of
Flight.

Early Morning

Across the road
Man coming
Down the hill with a
Rifle

I squint up my
Eyes.

Not rifle:
Chainsaw

Easier on a
Sunday morning
Hunting trees
Instead of
Rabbits.

Easter Lilies

February already:
Along the fence
A line of pink lilies
Long-legged chorus girls
In ruffled skirts.

End of November

All the bright colour
Has gone from the
Paddock grass.

Instead:

Delicate in the wind
Feathered seed heads

If Nature's first green is gold
So is her last.

Robert Frost wrote a poem beginning, 'Nature's first green is gold'.

Fantasy in Blue and Silver

I have found
At last
A magic place.

Dawn; and the
Striated sky
Reflected in the
Silver water.

Lilies.

A white bird wading.

Among the scattered
Rocks
Leap of a startled
Kangaroo.

Ghost gums.

Over to the west
The brolgas begin their
Dance
A slow undulation of
Elegant necks and
Unfurled wings.

Slowly
One by one the
Unicorn
Come down from the hills
To drink;
Each one defined
By its own aura
Of light.

First Week in September

Through my open door
A fall of
Light
Blue sky
A glimpse of pink blossom.

No birds at the feeder

Does this mean
Winter is over.

Fantasy in Red and Gold

She says,
'I don't want to talk any more.'
Watches the words
Coalesce
In her mind
Spheres of light in a
Darkening sky.

She says,
(Suddenly resolute)
'I don't want to
Listen either.'
Catches her breath
Wonder now
Explosion of
Red and orange
A trail of
Falling stars.

She shakes her head
Knows this is
Fantasy
But the colours
Dance inside her
As if they're real.

Fusion

She said,
Frowning,
Severe,
'Monarch butterflies
Are introduced.
You should not
Encourage them
To your garden.'

But…but…

I look around me

Spinebills busy
Among the trailing
Fuchsia.

Kookaburra on a
Fence post.

Skinks.

Under the silver birch
A blackbird
Sorting debris.

Oh! Oh!
Morning light
Transforming
My hollyhock flowers
Each petal
Stained glass:
Christ's passion.

This
All this

Mine to delight in.

Laratinga Wetlands

On the green water
Ducks

Nest in the reeds and
Two awkward-legged swamp
Hens

Wind

Thrum of frogs

Sudden flight of white
Corellas

Above the sombre hills
Sunset ending;
Trail of magenta clouds
Across a torn
Sky

Here
Here at last
Sanctuary

Rosellas

Meeting at Mylor
Nothing important
Window frames a
Square of
Dull sky and a
Leafless tree.

Sudden flash of wings
A pair of
Crimson rosellas.

Soon gone though

I turn back to the
Crowded room.

Everything's changed
I smile to myself
Greyness dissected
With red, yellow and
Blue.

Poem for the End of Love in November

for Gabrielle

I do not come
As a child
Pleading.

Only

Only

You gave me
A bird
To hold
Living
In my hands
And it has just
Died.

Acknowledgements

'The Quality of Light', *The Mozzie*, Volume 23, issue 6
'The Flowers You Sent Me', *The Mozzie*, Volume 20, issue 2
'Despair', *The Mozzie*, Volume 23, issue 9
'Almost Burnt-out Candle in a Moon Jar', *tamba* 57
'Sunday Drive: Early September', *Polestar* 30
'Gum Tree: Canberra', *The Mozzie*, Volume 24, issue 2
'Votive', *The Mozzie*, Volume 24, issue 8
'My Mind', 'The Rainbow Tree', *The Mozzie*, Volume 24, issue 3
Bedroom Curtains, *Positive Words*, April 2016
I Think, *tamba* 58
'For My Mother' and 'Poem for Lotte', *The Mozzie*, Volume 24, issue 7
'Poem for Elwin', *Positive Words*, August 2014
'Poem for Lotte', *The Mozzie*, Volume 24, issue 4
'At school', *The Mozzie*, Volume 23, issue 4
'Zebra Finches: Mt Barker Fodder Store', *The Mozzie*, Volume 24, issue 5
'Poem for Sonja' *The Mozzie*, Volume 23, issue 9
'On Buying a Bird Bath', *The Mozzie*, Volume 23, issue 8
'Rare Black Cockatoo', *The Mozzie*, Volume 22, issue 9
'Wild Oats', *The Mozzie*, Volume 24, issue 1
'Poem for Katherine Mansfield', *The Mozzie*, Volume 23, issue 1
'On Starting a New Jigsaw', *Positive Words*, April 2015
'Magpies', *Positive Words*, December 2009
'Turner: *The Bridge of Sighs*', *The Mozzie*, Volume 22, issue 10
'Beginning of September', *tamba* 55
'Early Morning', *The Mozzie*, Volume 23, issue 4
'Fantasy in Blue and Silver', *The Mozzie*, Volume 24, issue 8
'Fantasy in Red and Gold', *The Mozzie*, Volume 24, issue 10
'Fusion', *Polestar* 30
'Rosellas', *Positive Words*, October 2012

www.ingramcontent.com/pod-product-compliance
Lightning Source LLC
Chambersburg PA
CBHW062157100526
44589CB00014B/1862